TIMES PAST

THE STORY OF GLASGOW

Words by Russell Leadbetter

Picture Editing by Rod Sibbald

BLACK & WHITE PUBLISHING

First published 2004
by Black & White Publishing Ltd,
99 Giles Street, Edinburgh EH6 6BZ

Reprinted 2004

ISBN 1 84502 029 4

British Library Cataloguing in publication data: a catalogue record for this book is available from The British Library.

Printed and bound by Biddles Ltd

These photos, which are drawn from the *Evening Times* partwork TimesPast, can be purchased from the Photo Sales Department on 0141 302 7000.

Acknowledgements: Additional picture research by
Malcolm Beaton, Jim McNeish, Tony Murray and Eva Mutter

Contents

A three-year-old boy turning on the water for his sister at the drinking fountain in Queen's Park, Glasgow, in the less health conscious 1950s

GROWING UP

CHAPTER ONE

GROWING UP

HOLEY JUMPERS AND SKIPPING SCHOOL

It's not just Billy Connolly's fault, though he should take some of the blame. What is it about Glasgow childhoods – the single-ends, the backcourt games, the jeely pieces, the runny noses, the holey jumpers, the wellies worn in summer – that has made them seem so familiar even to people who grew up in other towns and cities?

Such images were presumably part of childhoods spent all across Scotland, yet they seem to typify Glasgow more than anywhere else. Billy's stage routines have made the Glasgow experience well known, of course, but a skip-load of novels, autobiographies and short stories, films and TV productions have also contributed.

As you read this, Glaswegians at home and abroad are logging on to websites to offer their recollections of living and growing up in the city. Glaswegians Reunited, so to speak.

It has to be said that there were many Glasgow childhoods that were far from deprived – it's difficult to imagine the children of the well-to-do merchants or university classes having to kill rats with pickaxe handles in the backcourts or waiting for jam sandwiches to be tossed down to them from the kitchen window.

So has the portrayal of deprivation been overdone? Not necessarily. The late George Friel (author of *The Boy Who Wanted Peace* and other books set in Glasgow's new housing schemes, tenements and run-down industrial centres during the 50s and 60s) was once asked why his fictional Glasgow world was so bleak.

He responded by saying, 'What am I to do? Put my head in the sand and say that everything is lovely? Surely a novelist, if he is writing about contemporary life in Glasgow or wherever, must tell the truth as he sees it.'

Which is what expat Scots like Phil Singer do when they talk about their Glasgow childhoods. Phil was born in England and came to Govan with his parents and younger sister when he was just three years old. When they first moved north, the family lived in the Linthouse Buildings off Govan Road, a rivet's throw from the shipyards. After a few years, the family moved once again – this time to the Gorbals and a room-and-kitchen in a tenement in Logie Street. Now living in Spokane, in Washington State, Phil works as a metallurgical engineer for the Honeywell Corporation. Lakes, forests and mountains surround the town. Montana is forty minutes drive away and it'll take you just two hours to drive to Canada. Travelling east brings you to Idaho and the Rocky Mountains. In every sense, it's far removed from his deprived

boyhood in Govan and the Gorbals during the mid 1950s. But it doesn't take much to induce pangs of nostalgia in him. He says:

> When I reflect back on those days long gone and the lifestyle I have now, it still has me in wonder. I can remember it as if it were yesterday – the holes in my trousers and all the rest of it . . .
> School, as I remember, was a daunting experience as truancy played a big role in my poor education. The fact that I did not attend school on many days was due to the fact that I had no shoes to wear. Wellies were the fashion despite the hot summer weather. The kids at school were very cruel – they'd laugh at you because they knew you didn't have a good pair of shoes to wear. Mine had holes in them. Stuffing paper and cardboard into them became an art to protect your feet from the wet. So the fear of embarrassment often led to my skipping school.

Truancy had its good points for Phil and other kids in the same position. As he says, they could roam the city. Their parents might not have been impressed by the truancy, but at least they had none of the fears and uncertainties that many of today's parents have when their children roam out of doors. 'The city,' says Phil, 'was our playground.' At the age of eight, he and his friends would jump on a bus or an Underground train and see how far they could get for free, or make their way to the Govan ferry and, once on the other side of the river, head for the park, or the museum at Kelvingrove. Even today he can't understand why a bunch of boys who were so obviously skipping school were rarely denied a trip on the ferry or entry to Kelvingrove.

Hunger and poverty were simply part of life during those times. Phil continues:

> We were accustomed to such hardship for we knew nothing better. But it's depressing to reflect on those times when we were so hungry. Some of the boys in our gang would wander the backcourts searching for old dried pieces of bread to eat. It sounds disturbing now, but we'd also drink the water from the puddles. It was a miracle that I didn't die from any diseases . . . My mum once told me that she'd have to stay up until midnight on many occasions to walk two miles while pushing a pram to the nearest bakery to buy bread. Apparently bread was much cheaper when bought at that time. She'd push the pram all the way there and back again. It would be filled with bread for those neighbours who needed it. They'd all take it in turns to fetch the bread.

Phil also recalls the rag-and-bone men who would drop by every so often. He once exchanged his cowboy outfit for a balloon and some crayons. His mum, not unreasonably, went ballistic, as the outfit had been a birthday present. She wasted no time in seeking out the rag-and-bone man

and getting the outfit back. Money couldn't be wasted just like that, after all. Phil even remembers 'us kids pouring water down the drains and watching the rats try to escape. We'd get paid for any rats we killed.'

FUN AND GAMES

It wasn't all misery though. For some children, libraries and museums opened the doors to new interests, many of which were to last a lifetime. And picture houses did big business – not for nothing was Glasgow once known as Britain's 'Cinema City'. Cowboy films were especially popular. When screen cowboy Roy Rogers and his horse Trigger visited Glasgow in February 1954, for a number of sold-out shows at the Glasgow Empire, he was mobbed by crowds of kids who were scarcely able to believe that a big-screen legend had materialised before them. It was the same when Fess Parker, who played Davy Crockett on TV in the 50s, visited the city.

The uniformed organisations, such as the Brownies and the Boys' Brigade, all had large memberships (the BB, after all, had started in Glasgow in 1883, courtesy of one William Smith). Charitable and other organisations frequently put on treats for children of deprived families.

Small kids played out on the streets and in the backcourts from dusk 'til dawn. Billy Connolly makes audiences laugh with the story of a neighbour, slightly the worse for wear, who was under instructions to round up his eight kids. Unable to find the full complement, he simply grabbed the young Billy and his sister Florence and chucked them into bed along with the others.

And, come rain or shine, the streets and the backcourts would ring to the sound of songs and rhymes. Joe Fisher lists some in his book, *The Glasgow Encyclopedia*. Here's a sample:

Oor wee school's the best wee school,
The best wee school in Glesca',
The only thing that's wrong wi' it
Is the baldy-heided maister.
He goes tae the pub on a Setturday night,
He goes tae church on Sunday,
And prays the Lord tae gie him strength
Tae belt the weans on Monday.

The late Glasgow singer-songwriter Matt McGinn wrote of his Calton childhood: 'As children we played in [Ross] Street at "Shops" and Release the Box and Kick the Can and cards and rounders and boxing and singing and peever and moshie and kicking doors after we'd tied them with string to some other neighbour's door and at guesses and at all kinds of races and we had to be good runners from the police who haunted the street.' Braver kids jumped the dykes, springing between middens or air-raid shelters. Footballs could be fashioned out of newspapers rolled up into a tight ball and fastened with string. Mud-pies could be made from, well, mud.

A GLASGOW CHRISTMAS

All the children looked forward to receiving real toys at Christmas but it wasn't until times of increased affluence that parents could really afford to splash out. In the decades before the Second World War, people often worked on Christmas Day and presents might take the shape of a stocking filled with fruit, a small toy and some chocolate, sometimes padded out with cinders. Clockwork engines and scooters were coveted and the lucky owners of the latter had a certain sort of status. A big treat was to get the tram into town and be taken to the shops and the Christmas decorations.

The war years and the post-war years were not exactly times of plenty, even at Christmas-time. But if you were a kid in the mid 50s, and if your parents had scraped together enough money, the gifts that could be bought from Wylie & Lochhead, the big store in Buchanan Street, included: walkie-talkie donkeys at £6 10s; a Big Top bagatelle at £1 10s 6d; and a genuine working model of a sewing machine at £3 4s 9d. A twenty-one-inch Pedigree doll that could walk and sit would have cost £8 11s. A new, three-wheeled pedal toy called an Autoscooter, with an adjustable saddle and handbrake, would have set Mum and Dad back £10 9s 6d. Lewis's store on Argyle Street was offering a Tri-ang PedalKar 350 for £3 2s 6d and a Tri-ang fort with ramp, drawbridge and sentry boxes for £1 10s 9d.

A WARTIME CHILDHOOD

The Second World War, of course, had prolonged effects on Glasgow's children, with its years of enforced rationing (some of which continued until July 1954), the disruption to schooling and everyday life, the hours spent huddled in shelters. In September 1939, thousands of children were taken from their families and evacuated to safer communities where, once they got over their homesickness, they could play in the fresh air. Others complained of their treatment and couldn't wait to return home. And in 1941 many children perished in the German bombings of Clydebank and parts of Glasgow.

The last century was often not kind to Glasgow children: shockingly high rates of infant mortality in the 1920s and 1930s, TB in the 1940s, grim overcrowding, poor sanitation and war. Today, however, sixty-five years after the onset of the war, the fortunes of Glasgow's increasingly multi-ethnic community of children have changed out of all recognition. Materially, most want for nothing – though too many of them still experience deprivation and other social problems. Will they, forty or fifty years hence, look back on their childhoods in the same nostalgic way as their parents and grandparents currently do to theirs?

People enjoying the Vinegarhill carnival, circa 1915

Joyce McChlery, 30 months, enjoys a free ride on her father's foot at Bingham's Pond, 1958

Learning about road safety in the playground of Hyndland School in 1948

Saturday in the snow,
Queens Park in the 1930s

Two young boys play with old newspapers and magazines in a doorway in the Gorbals in the 1950s

Street games in
the Gorbals, 1964

Making a splash at Gourock's outdoor pool in 1926

These are six of the ten children who were evicted from a condemned tenement in Shamrock Street in 1949

Councillor Pat Lally and Rev. Alastair Moodie of St. Paul's Church of Scotland, on a tour of deprived areas in Glasgow in 1975, pass kids playing on top of the remains of a mini-van

The view from Roystonhill towards the Red Road flats with children playing on the shell of a car, 1969

A little boy pouring his catch of minnows into a jam jar, Queens Park, 1951

Youngsters from the 'Western District' of Glasgow wearing their gas-masks during a mock attack, after the gas warning had been given. Practices like these were common in the early years of the war

Children playing on an improvised rope swing in a Glasgow back-court

These young evacuees were rescued from the ocean after being torpedoed in the middle of the night, but they look none the worse for wear

An unhappy youngster going on holiday at the Glasgow Fair in 1954

Construction work on Red Road Flats, Balornock

DAILY LIFE

Chapter Two

DAILY LIFE

TENEMENTS vs SCHEMES

Many Glasgow people were glad to put their years of tenement life behind them and to move into somewhere more spacious, whether it was in one of the New Towns or in one of the 'schemes', like Drumchapel or Easterhouse. It meant no more severe overcrowding, no more shared toilets, no more of the back-breaking work that came from taking your turn to scrub the stairs.

But there are others who, for all the drawbacks of tenement life, still miss the sense of togetherness. They recall how they would look out for one another, the handy shops and pubs on the corner, the kids playing on the streets until darkness fell. The post-war modernisation of the city's housing stock saw huge swathes of tenements disappearing to make way for new-builds and motorways but, in the process, a way of life that many older Glaswegians still have an affection for was torn up forever.

The late folk-singer Matt McGinn once vividly described his early life at 8 Ross Street, in the Calton. From both windows of the family's tenement home, he wrote, 'we had a magnificent view of a five-horse stable and, looming above it, the Ham Curer's with, as often as not, the thick black smoke belching from its windows to decorate the other buildings around.' As he describes it, his street, all 100 yards of it, was more like a village:

> there being in that tiny stretch two pubs and a sweetie shop, a joiner's and a blacksmith's shop, a garage and a Unitarian church which really had no right to be there because there wasn't a Unitarian in the street; there was a gasfitter and plumber's, a sausage-casing manufacturer's and a zoo, no less, which still left room for a high-class florist, a bookshop, the five-horse stable, a grocer's, the back-end of a foundry and a Women's Model Lodging House; and there were five hundred of us living in one-, two- and three-roomed houses in three-storey tenements.

GOOD NEIGHBOURS

There's been a persistent, shorthand view of Glasgow that goes: No Mean City, overcrowded tenements, squalor, gang violence . . . Well, yes, Glasgow has had to endure all of these and more, but the tenements were home to many thousands of families and, even though they were sometimes a bit cramped – it wasn't uncommon for families of ten or eleven to share two rooms –

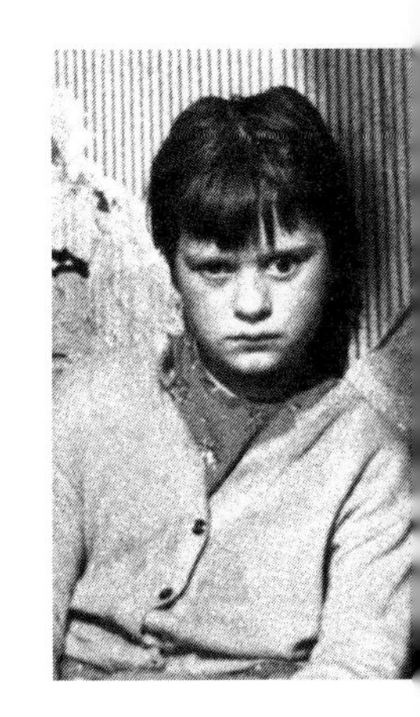

they were almost always cosy and clean. Cooking smells permeated the close. The sound of family life was never far away. People lent neighbours a helping hand. It was, in many ways, a community in microcosm.

'Socially, the tenement was a vertical village, and everyone knew everyone,' writes Pamela Stephenson in *Billy*, her biography of her husband, Billy Connolly. For the first three years of his life, Billy and his sister Florence slept in a curtained-off alcove in the kitchen of a tenement flat at 65 Dover Street, Anderston. The family bathed in the kitchen sink, and there was no hot water to speak of. It was so cramped that, to this day, writes Pamela, Billy gets uncomfortable whenever he finds himself in spacious accommodation. The Big Yin is far from being the only celebrity who experienced daily tenement life at first hand. Gerry Rafferty, his former partner in the Humblebums, spent his childhood years in a Paisley tenement before going on to make his fortune with songs like 'Baker Street'.

Best-selling author Meg Henderson's earliest memory stems from the day in June, 1951 – she was just four at the time – when her childhood tenement home, in Townhead, collapsed. She once recalled:

> After a long spell of warm dry weather the rain began bucketing. Our neighbour came down to tell my mother that there was dirt and sawdust coming through her walls and ceiling. My mum seemed to sense what was about to happen and started telling everyone to get out. Except she forgot about us – we were rescued by the fire brigade.

Comedian Arnold Brown has said of his Glasgow tenement upbringing:

> There were two bedrooms, one front room and a kitchen – and four of us. Everything was very cramped. The bathroom was a cubbyhole. We weren't rich but we weren't poor. One side of the landing had hot water and the other didn't and we were the side that had to go to the public baths. I thought there was some sort of God in the sky who said that side of the landing is the side that doesn't have hot water.

But the sense of community was especially strong in those days. Your playmates were next door or just up the stairs. Families shared communal cleaning duties – the toilets, the stairs – and woe betide those who shirked such duties. The shared toilets must have brought their own sense of community – as Billy Connolly once remarked, 'At least you were sure that the seat would always be warm.'

A VIEW FROM ACROSS THE POND

On the other side of the Atlantic, the tenements and their way of life evoke pleasant memories for Jean Faley, a university professor of Anthropology and Sociology in Wisconsin. She is from Glasgow and, before being uprooted and taken to America, spent her first sixteen years in a tenement. A decade or so ago, Jean edited a book, *Up Oor Close*, in which Glasgow people contributed memories of their tenement lives. She herself wrote:

> Our room-and-kitchen tenement house was cosy, clean and pretty. At night, in my little recessed bed, 'ben the room', I was lulled asleep by the sounds of the steam trains passing, the tinkling chimes of the Westminster clock, and the flames of the fire flickering on the wall.
>
> Over the years I have returned again and again in my mind's eye to that room, and the old kitchen with the big black fire, the recessed bed with its pretty rose-coloured bedspread and matching curtains, the sideboard with its doilies and ornaments, and the little gong rather grandly used to summon visitors from the room to tea in the kitchen of a Sunday afternoon. Ours was a well-regulated and orderly life . . .

These little details – the tea-time gong, the doilies – might suggest a family who lived a privileged life in the West End, but actually Jean's home was in Gourlay Street, in Springburn. She adds, for good measure, 'In many ways . . . mine was a typical tenement upbringing, representative of the majority of working-class tenement families. Not the merchant or University class, or their large mansion-like tenements, not the poorer working class who knew real destitution.'

KIDS TURN PEST CONTROLLERS

The voices in Jean's book fondly recall the warmth and friendliness of the tenements, of memorable Hogmanay parties, of the shared alarm and uncertainties during the years of the Blitz – of how, when a tenement dweller passed away, all the curtains would be closed.

Outside, in the backcourts and on the streets, kids would play and chant their songs or sit on the stairs on chilly winter nights and thrill each other with ghost stories. Jeely pieces would sometimes be thrown from upper-storey windows into waiting hands below. Sometimes, the kids would turn their energies to different pursuits – like the day in July, 1956, when a group of Gorbals boys armed themselves with pickaxes and wooden handles and set out to tackle the rats that were infesting Florence Street. Within hours, no fewer than 119 rats lay dead. One wee boy triumphantly told a reporter, 'I hadn't anything to hit them with, mister, so I got three with my feet!'

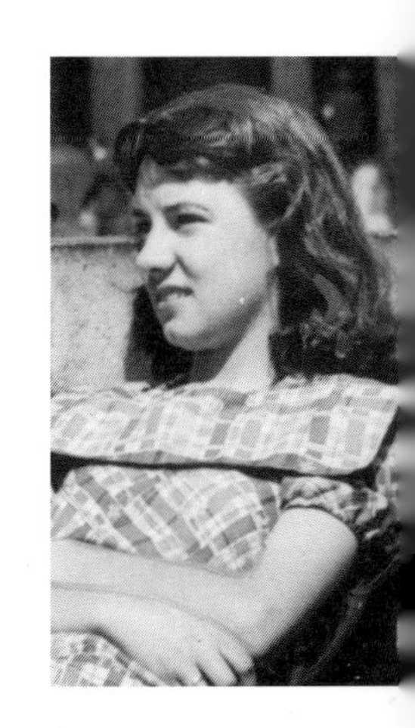

THE STEAMIES

Back then, a woman's work was, almost literally, never done. When it came to washing clothes for a big family, you either did it in the backcourt wash-house, having first boiled a large copper pot of water, or in the nearest steamie in one of the city's many swimming-baths. Clothes were bundled up and taken to and from the steamie in prams or in washing-baskets with wheels. The steamie was a good place to meet your friends and exchange gossip – hence the phrase, 'the talk of the steamie'. If you want to know what the steamies were like, there's still no better starting-point than Tony Roper's much-loved play *The Steamie*, which is now available in novel form.

SHOPPING

Day-to-day shopping tended to be done locally. This was not the era when the family would pile into the car and head for the twenty-four-hour Tesco superstore on Saturday mornings. This was the era of the Co-op, of Mrs Sancroft's tobacconist and newsagents in Gourlay Street, of the Andrew Cochrane chain of grocers, of Arnott's, of the D&F furniture store in the Gallowgate (Scotland's largest walk-round store, it was claimed). Some, though by no means all, local shops might offer you tick for a few days to see you through until the wages came through. There was no shortage of shops to choose from – it has been estimated that, by the 1930s, the Gorbals had 1,000 shops and 130 pubs serving an estimated 90,000 people.

BRING IN THE BULLDOZERS

But the tenements couldn't last. The city's housing stock had been neglected for too long and the worries about overcrowding and poor sanitation – thirty-seven per cent were still sharing a toilet as late as 1951 – had solidified into a desire to take remedial action. And so thousands of Glaswegian families were gradually relocated to New Towns like East Kilbride or to one of the great peripheral housing schemes – Drumchapel, Easterhouse, Castlemilk and Pollok – while huge redevelopment projects got underway in areas like Gorbals-Hutchesontown. The big schemes, of course, were to pose their own social problems in the 1980s. But many of the old tenements have survived to this day and, while few people would actively wish a return to the days of shared loos and serious overcrowding, there's no doubt that the tenement and its way of life have an uncanny ability to make many older people hanker for the past.

An apple seller has a cup of tea, 1949

A rag man pushing his cart in the Finnieston area of Glasgow, 1964

Spring flower sellers in Glasgow's Buchanan Street, 1963

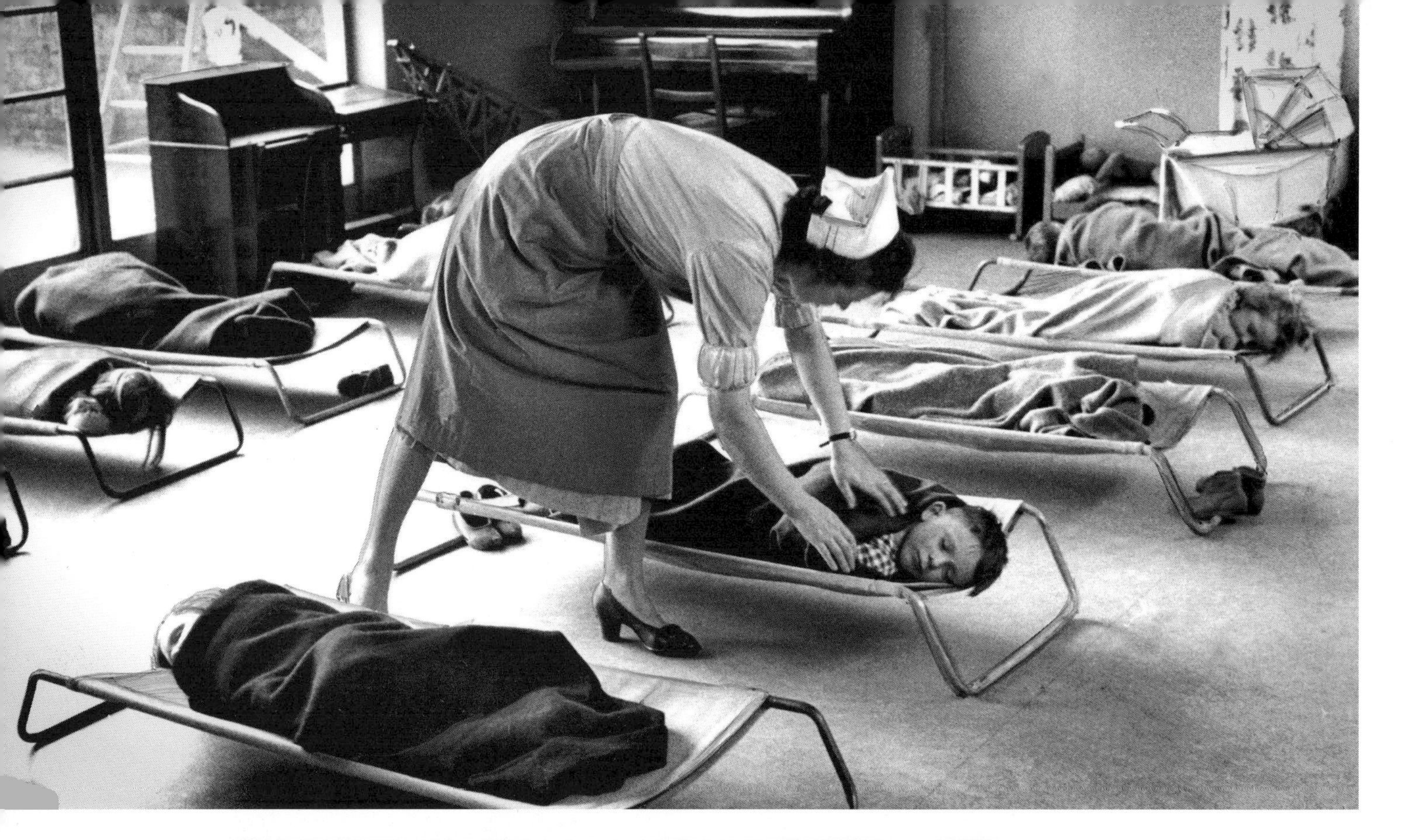

Douglas Street Day Nursery, 1958.
Children enjoy a post-lunch nap

This single-end was home to a family of eight. The facilities would not have been updated since the tenement was built and it is now 1964

A child sitting in a dishevelled bed in a damp room with peeling wallpaper in a Gorbals tenement, 1968

A chimney-sweep kisses the bride for luck, after her wedding to the local scoutmaster, in 1951

A three-year-old being bathed in the kitchen sink in the 1980s

A couple stroll through Glasgow's Royal Exchange Square in the winter of 1940

After a day at the sales, these women head for home, laden with rugs to brighten up the 1948 post-war gloom

Young women enjoy some lunchtime sun in George Square in the late 1940s

An evocative shot of Argyle Street in the 1950s

Catching up with the day's news

Flooding in Glasgow, 1954

Inspecting a fowl at the mobile fish shop, which was formerly an RAF ambulance

Hutchesontown tenements are demolished to make way for Sir Basil Spence's modern high-rise flats in the 1960s

Ghostly figures on the steps of Glasgow's Central Station in 1960

ON THE MOVE

CHAPTER THREE

ON THE MOVE

THE CAURS

Anyone who doubts that, beneath its no-nonsense exterior, Glasgow can be a sentimental city should have been present on 4 September 1962. A crowd estimated to have been in excess of 200,000 – more than a quarter of the population – gathered on the streets to bid a fond farewell to the trams, affectionately known as 'caurs'. It was one of those days when a bit of the city's history was slipping away forever but, while other cities might have been content to axe their trams with a swift and decisive action, and think no more about it, this being Glasgow, a final parade had to be arranged.

And, this being Glasgow, it was also a day of torrential rain, which only enhanced the sombre tone of the occasion. But the crowd was huge. Not even royalty could tempt so many people out of doors. Kids perched on their parents' shoulders in order to glimpse the trams. Among the older spectators, tears were often not far away. Streamers and hankies were waved. From every tenement in London Road and Dalmarnock Road, people were enjoying a 'hing' – leaning out of the windows. Near Glasgow Cross, a woman in a first-floor window raised her glass of beer in a salute.

The procession involved twenty trams of eight different types, one of them drawn by two white horses, on a three-mile journey along London Road, Trongate, Argyle Street, Hope Street, St Vincent Street, Union Street, Jamaica Bridge and Eglinton Toll. Dignitaries from Glasgow and elsewhere in Britain sat in the trams and waved to the crowds. It was, wrote one correspondent, 'one of the most affecting Glasgow scenes for many years'. True to form, the eighth tram broke down in London Road, causing a snarl-up of all those behind it – something that had happened frequently in the city's streets for real.

The trams were part of Glasgow life for ninety years and sixteen days, having been launched in August 1872. Then, too, a large crowd had gathered to watch the inaugural procession of seven horse-drawn trams on rails, civic dignitaries again on board.

None of the routes was longer than three miles, and all radiated from the city centre. The penny tickets were white, the twopenny red and the threepenny blue. To stop a horse-drawn tram, you simply waved one down. If the driver didn't see you, the guard would pull a leather thong and a bell would tinkle above the driver's head. The horses would hear it and prepare to slow down and the driver would apply the brake.

In 1894, following a protracted row, Glasgow Corporation took over the trams from the

Glasgow Tramway Company, which had leased the road rights from the city. The Corporation made a little bit of British history by becoming the first to own and operate a public transport system. Joe Fisher, in *The Glasgow Encyclopedia*, says that it had 384 horse-drawn cars, 3,000 horses, nine depots and thirty-one miles of track. Horsepower gave way to electric traction in time for the International Exhibition at Kelvingrove in May 1901.

The trams were hugely popular but, after their peak, they fell into a slow decline. Contributory factors, says Fisher, included Glasgow's expansion, steep tram fares, and growing competition from buses. By 1948, the city had more than 1,000 trams but the writing was on the wall and services began to be cut, ending in a straggle of surviving routes. The final procession on 4 September 1962 saw them disappear forever.

As more than one writer observed at the time, the trams were as much a part of Glasgow as Rangers or Celtic. Memories poured forth in print, evoking the distinctive smell and rattling noise of the trams, the interior doors that would slam open and shut at speed, the medieval-looking chains that kept would-be passengers from boarding when the trams were full. The week before the parade, Glaswegians bought themselves a tenpence ride from Auchenshuggle (yes, it does exist!) to Dalmuir, one last journey before the caurs were scrapped. 'What I'll miss,' said one teacher on board, 'is the noise of them late at night. You could hear them booming along for miles, and it was a pleasant sound.'

One woman told how she used the slow-moving trams to window-shop and would jump out whenever she saw anything she liked. Schoolboys came up from places like Leeds, armed with cine cameras, just so they could say that they had got the tram to Auchenshuggle. 'We get some wi' cameras every trip these past few days,' one conductress said, adding, 'Ah've had my picture taken three times today.'

A new generation of buses were taking the place of the trams, though this conductress and others were sceptical. 'Ah'm dreadin' thae buses,' she confided. 'If something goes wrong wi' a tram the conductor can aye stop it wi' the brake at the back – but whit can ye dae wi' a bus?'

A week later, during the procession, thousands of cameras flashed in the gloom in every street the departing trams passed. Hundreds of people risked limbs by placing a coin on the tracks for a commemorative flattening.

People had come from miles around to be here, and there was chaos on the roads. Some motorists, keen to have more than one look at the trams, drove ahead and tried to head them off, which didn't improve the tempers of the police-officers who were trying to control the proceedings.

At Hope Street, some boys set off a large firecracker as the Lord Provost's tram passed. 'My Goad,' cried one woman, 'it's blew up!' As the procession reached Eglinton Toll, the heavens opened. 'Here', wrote one journalist, 'the trams were given their final send-off, with the deafening chorus of hundreds of motor-horns from motorists waiting to see the trams' last shoogle into Coplawhill'.

By mistake, a Corporation bus wandered into the stately procession and sent ripples of dismay among the watchers.

Soon after the procession, the last rails were ripped up. A handful of trams were sent to museums at home and abroad, some of them to Glasgow's own Museum of Transport. As you read this, you can be sure that a Glaswegian of a certain age will be standing in front of them, gently reliving the memories of the sounds and smells of the tram.

THE BLUE TRAIN AND THE CLOCKWORK ORANGE

Apart from the bus, a new electric suburban railway with 150 miles of track – the Blue Train – was advertising itself in 1962 to commuters. And there was always the Underground. Another invention from the Victorian era, it is still going strong. It was opened in 1896, making it the third oldest in the world after London and Budapest. Its fifteen stations were served by a 10.4-km-long double track circular route. Originally built by the private sector, it passed into public ownership as part of Glasgow Corporation Transport in 1923. In 1977, it shut down for a huge three-year modernisation. Today Glasgow's underground system, known to all as the Clockwork Orange because of the colour of its livery, carries more than fourteen million passengers a year.

THE TROLLEYBUS

Another means of getting about the city was the trolleybus. It had made its first appearance in 1949 and combined the advantages of both bus and tram. Because of its ability to materialise behind you without a sound, it was nicknamed the 'Silent Death'. Trolleybuses were gradually phased out, and the last one ran in 1967.

THE RAILPLANE

George Bennie's Railplane was an ambitious scheme, ahead of its time, but ultimately failed to get off the ground. The Railplane was an experimental luxury coach, slung under a double track thirty feet above rail lines and powered by an electric motor turning propellers at front and back. At speeds of 120 mph, it would be able to transport passengers from Glasgow to Edinburgh in under twenty minutes. On 8 July 1930, in a field in Milngavie, hundreds of people witnessed the Railplane's first trip. Public interest was huge, but the scheme withered and died for want of financial backing: not surprising, maybe, at a time of recession and growing unemployment. Who knows what would have happened if banks and other investors had been able to put their hands in their pockets?

A tram negotiates a right turn from Great Western Road into Kirklee Road, a notorious accident blackspot at the time, 1937

A steam engine crosses the Clyde beside Jamaica Bridge, Glasgow in 1950

The King's Theatre as it looked in the 1920s. The Wolseley car was used on stage in a show called *Out to Win*

Departures information 1933-style. The station announcer at Queen Street Station alerts passengers to train information

Easter Monday at St Enoch Station, Glasgow: the Saltcoats and Largs train all ready to go – and eager holiday-makers rushing to secure seats, 1955

Glasgow subway in 1964, prior to modernisation

A snow scene at the junction of Argyle Street, Oswald Street and Hope Street in the 1950s, showing trams, cars and a hand-cart in front of the Heilan'mans Umbrella

The stairs to Buchanan Street subway station, 1965

£1500
PLACE
THE BALL
EVENING
TIMES
DINO'S

Glasgow traffic on Jamaica Bridge in 1955

Huge crowds gather to watch the last tram parade in Glasgow in 1962

Trams give way to a horse and cart on a foggy day in the early 1960s

Reading the newspaper on a Glasgow tram, 1962

Collecting the fares on a Glasgow tram, 1962

A long wait after the match beckons for those parked in the Hampden Park car park in 1952

Motorists struggle through the snow in St Enoch's Square, 1952

Stacks of wood pulp at Clyde Paper Mills, 1935

INDUSTRY

CHAPTER FOUR

INDUSTRY

DECLINE

In 1971, the year after Ted Heath kicked Harold Wilson out of Downing Street, a Glasgow MP, Frank McElhone, rose to his feet in the Commons. There was no mistaking the urgency of his message. He said the city was now seen as Scotland's industrial graveyard rather than its industrial capital. Some 38,000 men were out of work, more than at any time since 1945. 'As a proud Glaswegian,' he continued, 'I feel bitterly angry and ashamed to see in this city so many gaunt monuments in the form of hundreds of empty factories, workshops and yards.' Fixing the government front-benches in his sights, he firmly pinned the blame on ministers. Just as robustly, the ministers denied any such responsibility.

There was no doubt that British industry was going through a rough time. The industrial strife of the late 1960s under Wilson had helped Heath to election victory in June, 1970, but within a month troops were being put on standby as a national dock strike got underway. By November, it was reported that there had been a record 8.8 million days lost through strike action that year. In 1971, postal workers went on strike for the first time, Rolls Royce went bankrupt, 1.5 million workers staged one-day strikes over a new industrial relations bill and the government shut the door on the 'lame duck' of the Upper Clyde Shipbuilders consortium. The following year, a miners' strike led to three-day weeks and power blackouts.

McElhone's Glasgow, the one-time city of industry, had been transferred to the intensive care ward. The home of St Rollox, of North British Locomotive, of William Beardmore, of Sir William Arrol, was now a pale and sickly shadow.

Glasgow and the West of Scotland had specialised in the heavy industries – coal, metal manufacture, shipbuilding and mechanical engineering – which, from the 1870s right up to the immediate post-war era, had been the powerhouse of Scotland. But too many of them had been in a long and steady decline and, for various reasons, had been too slow to make the radical changes they needed to survive in an increasingly fast-changing world.

THE SECOND CITY OF THE EMPIRE

In the late eighteenth and nineteenth centuries, Glasgow had shown remarkable enterprise in exploiting natural resources and creating new markets. The quantity of tobacco and cotton and

linen textiles being exported reaching quite phenomenal levels. Textile manufacturing became a key employer, as did iron-founding, and coal-mining. By the 1830s, Glasgow's manufacturing activities included almost every industry imaginable. It had the world's biggest chemical works, at St Rollox, which employed 1,000 workers.

This was an era of the entrepreneur. One, William Beardmore, took his grandfather's business and propelled it to dizzying new heights. In the words of Kenneth Hurst's recent book on the Empire, the multi-disciplinary business expanded to include 'steelmaking, heavy forgings, rolling mills, armour plate, naval guns, battleships, passenger liners, marine diesels . . . aircraft, airships, aero engines, high-speed diesel engines, steam locomotives, six separate cars, four different makes of commercial vehicles, and two different motorcycle and motorcycle engine companies in ten different factories'. The huge Parkhead Forge boasted an enormous steam hammer known as Samson, the relentless noise of which could be heard for miles around.

William Beardmore – later Lord Invernairn – was a visionary. He was not the first and certainly not the last to emerge from Glasgow and the West, but he was a flawed businessman, and made mistakes. By the mid 1920s, the company was all but bankrupt and Beardmore was stripped of his executive responsibilities. He suffered (as so many others did) during the Depression and, according to Hurst, when William died in 1936, 'the financial affairs of his estate were so complicated that it took three years to sort them out'.

Another far-sighted pioneer was Sir William Arrol, who opened the Dalmarnock Iron Works in 1887. He turned the art of bridge-building on its head. His idea? Build the structure on dry land then roll it out, span by span, into the area to be bridged. Simple yet brilliantly effective. His masterpiece was the Forth Rail Bridge, which was completed in 1889. Known for a time as the eighth wonder of the world, it earned him a knighthood. His other achievements as a contractor included the steelwork for London's Tower Bridge, the Wear Bridge in Sunderland and several bridges over the Nile. He built the slipway gantry at the Belfast shipyard of Harland and Wolff, beneath which the Titanic was constructed. His London company built the Battersea and Bankside power stations – today the latter is the home of the Tate Modern Gallery. When he died, his Dalmarnock premises were said to be the UK's biggest girder construction works, occupying some twenty acres and employing between 4,000 and 5,000 men.

In the late Victorian era, Glasgow's expertise in industry and commerce had made it a self-confident city and many ornate buildings were erected to match this. The City Chambers, with its stunning facade, reflected this prosperous attitude perfectly. The city might have had lots of social problems but civic pride was buoyant – something that was illustrated by the great Exhibitions of 1888 and 1901.

It hadn't all been plain sailing during the Victorian era. Recessions had had to be endured, and too much of the local economy was dependent on shipbuilding, a volatile business, but Glasgow's industries still entered the twentieth century in generally good shape. Alongside the basic heavy industries were the smaller, but just as important, ones like agricultural chemicals, food and drink manufacturing, potteries and paper-related industries.

INTO THE TWENTIETH CENTURY

In 1903, there was another major success story – the North British Locomotive Company. It was the result of an amalgamation of three enterprising firms – Neilson Reid and Co. Dubs and Co. and Sharp Stewart and Co. each of which had a long history of locomotive-building for railways in Britain and around the world.

NB would become a world-famous name in locomotive engineering. Its workshops in Springburn and Queens Park turned out locos at the rate of 450 a year between 1903 and 1914, bound for Paraguay, India and Russia, and every country in between. A small number may even be in operation today.

The First World War and the urgent need to re-arm were good news for Glasgow industry, and, even when the war was over, there seemed to be few clouds on the horizon, with the motor-car industry anticipating a booming uninterrupted future.

Socially, however, things had changed. The war meant that large numbers of women entered the national workforce. There had also been signs of growing industrial unrest during the war years, which would eventually give rise to the myth of 'Red Clydeside'.

The war years had seen a number of rent and industrial strikes in the city, then on 31 January 1919, a vast crowd of workers assembled in George Square, the Red Flag flying above their heads, in pursuit of their demand for a forty-hour working week. At a time of mounting unemployment, and with thousands of soldiers returning from the front, they believed a forty-hour week was the fairest solution. According to contemporary first-hand reports, some strikers refused to make way for trams running past the Square, prompting a baton-charge by police, which itself gave rise to pitched battles. The Scottish Secretary, Robert Munro, scenting a 'Bolshevik rising', despatched tanks into the Square and 12,000 troops to quell the unrest. The strike leaders were arrested.

Meantime, many overseas countries had been sharpening their expertise in shipbuilding, coal and heavy machinery, which was to have a knock-on effect on Glasgow's industrial fortunes. When the post-war slump in world trade kicked in, Glasgow was caught unawares and suffered badly. Shipbuilding took a body blow – and, since it was served by so many ancillary industries, these, too, paid the price when the yards went silent. Over the next few years, the Depression

made things even worse. North British Locomotives, for example, made no locomotives whatsoever in 1932. The interwar years were bleak for Glasgow and for Scotland. The country didn't have much luck in attracting the new growth industries, many of which went to England instead. The population was shrinking and joblessness stood at crippling levels.

AFTER WORLD WAR II

But the re-armament of the closing years of the 1930s was a boost for the shipyards and for heavy engineering companies. There was a boom after 1945, too, but Glasgow seemed to be relying too much on the traditional heavy industries that had served it so well for so long. The writing already seemed to be on the wall. In 1952, Glasgow's Lord Provost, Sir Victor Warren, voiced his fears about the future of Glasgow's economy because of a lack of raw materials. Even without strikes, he predicted, many people would find themselves out of a job. Not many people seemed to have listened to him. Or maybe it was because the damage had already been done and it was too late for radical measures. Heavy industry had not done a very good job in diversifying or re-investing. One by one, the big names closed down. North British Locomotives went into liquidation in 1962, its workforce having been slashed from 5,000 to just 1,500.

In the post-war era, Scotland succeeded in attracting American and Japanese-owned branch factories but sometimes even they seemed volatile.

Over the last decade or two, Scotland has suffered numerous high-profile closures, from Ravenscraig, Caterpillar and Singer to Goodyear, Hoover and the car-making plant at Linwood, but it has responded by diversifying and seeking new fields. Scottish industry today is one that our Victorian forefathers would struggle to recognise.

Towering smoke stacks dominate this scene in Motherwell circa 1912

The rush hour in the late 1920s on the recently opened George V Bridge

Kirkintilloch, Dunbartonshire – pouring molten metal at the iron foundry in 1970

10

Paisley mill workers in good humour at the end of their shift in 1954

Sheltering from the heat at Ravenscraig Steel Works in the 1960s

The locomotive *Union of South Africa* at a St Rollox engineering works open day

Munitions production at the Bishopton Scottish Ordnance factory, 1940

A final brush before despatch: Templeton's carpet factory in the 1930s

Hillman Imp car bodies on the Rootes' assembly line, 1960s

Mounted police face up to pickets outside Ravenscraig during the miners' strike in 1984

Sir Charles Connell watches as the bulk carrier *Stonepool* is launched at Connell's shipyard in 1968

SHIPBUILDING

Chapter Five

SHIPBUILDING

H V MORTON'S VIEW OF THE CLYDE SHIPYARDS

At their peak, the shipyards of the Clyde must have been an awesome sight.

Back in the late 1920s, the popular travel writer H V Morton visited Glasgow as part of a tour of Scotland. He wrote:

> In a few miles, I see twenty, perhaps thirty, ships in their cradles, some just keels, like the skeleton of a whale in a museum; others gaunt hulls, rusty red or smeared with vermilion paint; a few almost ready for a bottle of champagne, and one the *Duchess of York*, terribly young and inexperienced, lying in dock with years of the Atlantic Ocean ahead of her . . . And the sound of the Clyde is that of a thousand hammers echoing in the empty belly of a hull; the fiendish chatter of electric riveters and a sudden squeal of metal tortured in the service of the seas. When I look up I see tiny men in flying cradles pressed against a mountain of steel-plate, hitting a white-hot rivet with a hammer, and at each stroke a million gold sparks fly hissing earthward to die of cold as they fall . . .
>
> If you have never seen the launching of a ship there is still a thrill in life for you.

He then went on to detail the excitement of seeing the immense shape of a ship sliding backwards and hitting the water for the first time.

Yet this was during a period, between the two world wars, when the shipyard industry had been suffering terribly. After the First World War, the government had cut back on arms spending and this, coupled with the onset of a recession, had marked effects on the yards along the Clyde.

Morton saw this for himself when he returned north a year or so later for another book, *In Scotland Again* (1933), in which he refers to the 'tragically silent state of the Clyde'. Many yards had had to be shut and, as the Great Depression took hold, the Clyde's output slumped from 600,000 tons in 1928 to a catastrophic 56,000 in 1933. Unemployment, naturally, increased too. Labour Exchanges were inundated with men looking for work. The Second City of the Empire, a title bestowed on Glasgow around the turn of the century, was beginning to look a little out-of-date.

Much of the city's industrial fortunes had longed hinged on shipbuilding, an industry which, at its height, took the city's name all over the world. It isn't difficult to see why the yards and their workers, and the ships that were built there, have entered Glasgow mythology and given Glasgow some of its most enduring images.

IN THE BEGINNING . . .

The story of shipping on the Clyde stretches back at least to 1812, when one Henry Bell launched the river's first commercial steamer service, *The Comet*. It was a success, making the route from Glasgow to Greenock much more popular than it had previously been.

Wooden ships had been the norm until the 1830s and 1840s, when they gave way to iron ships thanks to the efforts of far-sighted builders like Robert Napier, the partnership of David Tod and John McGregor, and others. Yards began to proliferate on the banks of the Clyde, including Fairfield's and Alexander Stephen's. By the 1880s, steel had begun to replace iron, and numerous ancillary industries sprang up to service the making of the ships.

The Clyde continued to expand at an impressive rate, to the extent that, in 1913, according to a report in the *Glasgow Herald*, its twenty miles of river produced 374 ships with a combined tonnage of 764,784. This was something of a golden age. Author Irene Maver says that, between 1860 and 1918, Glasgow was truly the world's shipbuilding capital.

SHIPBUILDING AND THE TWO WORLD WARS

The First World War was another spur to growth but then, as we have seen, there was a slump in the 1920s. In the downsizing that followed, not even the big shipbuilding names escaped. John Brown & Co at Clydebank, who had given the world such notable Cunard liners as *Lusitania* and *Aquitania*, as well as the battlecruisers *Inflexible* and *Hood*, was forced, in late 1931, to suspend work on a prestigious project, No 534, on which it had pinned so many hopes. The project was within sight of completion when the regretful letters were sent out to the workforce. The hulk of the unfinished ship, the largest ever to have been assembled on the Clyde, could be seen for miles around during the years of inactivity, a painful daily reminder of the Depression.

It wasn't until April 1934 that the yard, with government aid, was able to give workers the go-ahead to finish the project. Five months later, on 26 September, a day made miserable by grey skies and rain, the ship was launched, watched by an estimated 250,000 people. The *Queen Mary*, as it was now known, had finally reached the waters of the Clyde, though another year-and-a-half of completion work lay in store before it could finally go into service.

Shortly after the *Queen Mary*'s maiden voyage to New York, in May 1936, John Brown's won the contract for another grand Cunard liner. Project number 552 would set sail as the *Queen Elizabeth*. It was launched on 27 September 1938 and, by this time, Brown's and other yards were enjoying the full benefits of rearmament, as the government responded to Hitler's aggression in Europe. Brown's was probably not alone in being able to boast of full employment on the day war was finally declared, in September 1939.

THE YARDS IN THEIR DECLINING YEARS

After the war, however, it was a different story – one of gradual decline. In the 1950s, British shipbuilding found itself being increasingly overtaken by yards in the Far East and Europe.

In Glasgow, uncompetitive yards struggled to meet the new realities. The Harland & Wolff yard closed in 1963, one of several UK yards to fall silent in the early 1960s. But in December 1964 John Brown was relieved to be able to sign a contract for yet another Cunard liner, Number 736, better-known as the *QE2*. It would give the yard enough work for three years.

Harold Wilson's Labour government had been looking at ways of easing the crisis facing British shipbuilding, and the collapse, in 1965, of the Clyde yard of Fairfield's was a nasty reminder of how urgent the task had become. (Fairfield's was later bought over and restarted in what was known as 'the Fairfield experiment', boasting new yard techniques and a fresh approach to industrial relations.) Another famous Clyde yard, Barclay Curle, shut in 1968.

The official Geddes Report led, on the Clyde, to the creation of two consortia – Scott-Lithgow, on the lower reaches of the river, and the Upper Clyde Shipbuilders, comprised of Fairfield's, Yarrow's, Stephen's, Connell's and John Brown's, with some 13,000 workers in all. Brown's scrambled to finish the *QE2* on time and it was launched to great fanfare on 20 September 1967, less than five months before the official birth of UCS. But technical problems with the *QE2* turbines created considerable headaches and unwelcome publicity for UCS. Other factors conspired to land the UCS board in a number of serious financial crises, forcing them to go cap-in-hand several times from the government's Shipbuilding Industry Board. The long-term outlook was anything but rosy.

By the time of Edward Heath's victory over Wilson in the June 1970 general election, Yarrow's was poised to pull out of the UCS consortium and go back to private ownership. The UCS cash problems showed no signs of abating and the Tories finally pulled the plug on UCS after a year in power. UCS went into liquidation – but the embittered workforce had other ideas. It refused point-blank to accept closure, and staged a work-in that attracted worldwide sympathy and publicity.

'The closure of all the UCS yards would have been an economic disaster,' Jimmy Reid, a leading UCS shop steward, said a few years ago. 'We discussed that and made sure that everybody in the yards understood it. We also projected into the public consciousness the fact that economic decisions should not be taken in isolation from their social consequences.' In the end, the Tories realised they had to find ways to redeploy the UCS yards.

THE FUTURE OF CLYDESIDE

That was thirty-odd years ago. Today, shipbuilding on the Clyde is concentrated on just two yards, Scotstoun and Govan, both owned by BAE Systems. The Clyde, by and large, has fallen silent.

There is an old saying to the effect that Glasgow made the Clyde and the Clyde made Glasgow. In 2004, it is difficult to gaze down the waterfront and to try to visualize what H V Morton saw, back in the late 1920s. Huge new developments promise to bring life back to the Clyde, though they're not the kind of projects the shipbuilding pioneers could ever have foreseen. Glasgow has had to adapt to new global realities, reinventing itself to cope with the loss of shipbuilding and other heavy industries. But nothing can erase the image of those huge liners and warships taking shape in the yards and reminding people that, come launch day, there was still a thrill in life for them.

Shipyard workers returning to work on the *Queen Mary* after their lunch break

Crowds with umbrellas pack the shipyard in the pouring rain to watch the launch of the *Queen Mary* in 1934

The Clyde Trust's new crane at Finnieston Quay in 1932

QUEEN MARY

Spectators head for home after watching the *Queen Mary* begin her journey to the sea, March 1936

A worker prepares for a shift at the John Brown shipyard, 1964

Workers at the John Brown shipyard, in front of the partially built *QE2*, in 1967

An official of the AEU addressing a meeting at Fairfield's engine shop, 1965

The John Brown shipyard in Clydebank gets ready to build the *Queen Mary* in the early 1930s

Launch of the 18,500 ton *Ruahine* built for New Zealand at John Brown shipyards in Clydebank, 1950

The *QE2* makes her way down the Clyde in 1968

The *QE2* slides down the slipway at John Brown's shipyard in 1967

The *QE2* entering the dry dock at Greenock, 1968

The end of a shift at Barclay Curle shipyard in Glasgow in 1955

ÑEVASA
RE S.W.L. 10 CWTS

Miss Parker, an ATS enemy-aircraft spotter, with sunglasses and binoculars

CITY AT WAR

CHAPTER SIX

CITY AT WAR

THE INITIAL DAYS

The autumn of 1939 saw Europe brace itself for war. Hitler's aggressive territorial ambitions, which had already seen him occupy Austria and subjugate Czechoslovakia, had now swept him into Poland, which Britain had pledged to defend. Every attempt to appease him having failed, British Prime Minister Neville Chamberlain issued Hitler with an ultimatum – 'Remove your forces from Polish soil or face the consequences.' War now seemed unavoidable. Europe had been mobilising. The UK had been readying its economy for a lengthy war from the summer of that year and had also laid down wide-ranging plans for civil defence.

On Sunday, 3 September, the deadline for Chamberlain's ultimatum expired and Britain found itself at war for the second time in twenty-one years. The King took to the radio to broadcast to his people, urging them to stand calm, firm and united. The first blackout of the war occurred that same night. Low rain clouds obscured the moon and the darkness in Glasgow was total. Some people ventured in from the suburbs to see what the city looked like in wartime conditions. Constables and ARP (air-raid precautions) wardens toured backcourts to ensure that every tenement was dark.

Sunday had not yet given way to Monday when the first casualty of the war occurred. The Glasgow liner *Athenia*, bound for Canada with no fewer than 1,400 people on board, was torpedoed by a U-boat 300 miles beyond the Hebrides. One hundred and twelve people – possibly more – died. The survivors, soaked in dirty oil and water, were brought back either to Scotland, landing at the Clyde, or to Galway on the west coast of Ireland. Many of them were American, so the US Ambassador to Britain, Joseph Kennedy, sent his son north to greet them at Glasgow's Central Hotel. The young man, John F Kennedy, would later become the 35th President of the USA.

EVACUATION

Government ministers had already made the mass evacuation of children a national priority. During the opening days of that fateful September, an estimated 170,000 people – school-age children on their own and pre-school children with their mums – from congested and densely populated areas of Glasgow were transported out of harm's way, to Perthshire, Ayrshire, Stirlingshire, Aberdeen and the south of Scotland. Some merely went across the city to quieter suburbs.

From his office in Bath Street, the city's evacuation officer, a Mr Allardyce, placed advertisements telling parents that, on the day of evacuation, they should ensure their children were equipped with items including:

A Gas Mask
A Change of Underclothing
Night Clothes
House Shoes or Rubber Shoes

The notices added, however, 'No child desiring evacuation will be prevented from attending through lack of any of the above articles.'

Many children were to relish their new lives in the countryside, away from the teeming tenements, and they often made new friends in the process. But there were cases when the clash of different cultures led to all sorts of friction.

SAFETY FIRST

While the evacuations were being carried out, workmen were busy erecting corrugated-steel Anderson shelters, strengthening tenement closes with struts and digging trenches in parks; meanwhile, Glaswegians tried to get used to their gas masks. Lord Provost Patrick Dollan publicly praised their steadfastness and urged them to maintain their 'calm strength' and to follow regulations.

In the event, nothing much happened that September or in the months that followed during the so-called 'phoney war' at home. There were isolated incidents, though, like the German sinking of the battleship *HMS Royal Oak*, in Scapa Flow, with the loss of more than 800 lives, on 14 October.

FIGHTING TALK

Britain could only watch as Germany and Russia, which in August 1939 had signed the Molotov-Ribbentrop non-aggression pact, ran riot in Eastern Europe. In April 1940, Germany seized Denmark and then set its sights on Norway. Britain tried to intervene in Norway but it proved to be a disaster. It was Chamberlain's undoing. His gamble in seeking a vote of confidence in the Commons backfired, and he resigned. On 10 May, with the Nazi blitzkrieg overrunning Belgium and the Netherlands, sixty-four-year-old Winston Churchill stepped into the breach. 'I have nothing to offer but blood, toil, tears and sweat,' he told the country. His stirring speeches on radio and in Parliament led one US commentator to observe that he 'mobilised the English language and led it into battle.' Harry Benson, a Glasgow teenager who would grow up to become one of the world's best-known photojournalists, was inspired by Churchill's oratory to imagine himself as a top photographer at the centre of great world events. The Premier had that sort of effect on people.

On 4 June in the Commons, Churchill announced:

Even though large tracts of Europe and many old and famous States have fallen or may fall into the grip of the Gestapo and all the odious apparatus of the Nazi rule, we shall not flag or fail. We shall go on to the end, we shall fight in France, we shall fight on the seas and oceans, we shall fight on the beaches, we shall fight on the landing grounds.

But the Germans were pressing closer to the English Channel. The Allies were no match for them in France, and nearly 340,000 British and French troops had to be evacuated from Dunkirk so that they could fight another day. Paris surrendered on 14 June, by which time Italy had also declared war on us. Now Britain faced the enemy alone. 'Let us therefore brace ourselves to our duties,' Churchill urged Parliament on 18 June, 'and so bear ourselves that, if the British Empire and its Commonwealth last for a thousand years, men will still say, "This was their finest hour".'

THE BOMBING OF GLASGOW

Hitler's planned invasion of Britain foundered against the pilots of the RAF who, between mid July and mid September of 1940, brilliantly denied the Luftwaffe supremacy of the skies. The Germans attacked coastal shipping and fighter airfields before turning their attention to London, but by 15 September the RAF had won a stunning victory in the air over southern England, moving Churchill to declare, 'Never in the field of conflict, was so much owed by so many to so few.' Hitler was forced to look elsewhere, but his bombers continued to target Britain in a bid to destroy key ports and industrial centres and to undermine civilian morale.

On the morning of 19 July, 1940, the first daylight bombs fell on Glasgow, in Yoker and in Benburb. On 18 September there was the first night-time raid: one bomb damaged a warehouse at the corner of Queen Street and Ingram Street, while another exploded between the decks of a cruiser berthed at Yorkhill Quay, leading to the evacuation of the Sick Children's Hospital and hundreds of tenements.

The raids continued into the following year. Clydebank and parts of Glasgow suffered catastrophic damage on the nights of March 13-14 and 14-15, with some 1,200 people being killed, and only seven out of 12,000 Clydebank houses remaining undamaged. One Glasgow man recalled years later, in the book, *Scotland's War*: 'The incendiaries started coming down and it was like looking at falling flares or rain that was on fire. If you are eight years old when you're seeing this happening, it's like some kind of horror film.'

Amid the devastation and the despair, rescue squads found a boy of fifteen and a girl of eleven in the wreckage of a tenement. Both had been trapped for two days but emerged alive. The boy had sustained himself on a bag of sugar that had, by chance, been thrown into his bed from a cupboard when his home collapsed.

Further raids on Glasgow took place on 7-8 April, while on 5-7 May, Paisley and Greenock were the Luftwaffe's targets. On 10 May, Rudolf Hess, Hitler's deputy, baled out of a plane and landed in a field in Eaglesham, in a bizarre attempt to seek peace with Great Britain (one historian claims Hess was acting on the orders of Hitler, who'd been duped by a British Intelligence sting that a government faction would overthrow Churchill and negotiate peace with the Germans). Whatever the truth of the situation, Hess ended up in Spandau prison in Berlin, where he died in 1987.

GLASGOW – 'THE ARSENAL OF THE EMPIRE'

Glasgow and the West of Scotland were by now fully geared up for the war effort. Thousands of men had volunteered to fight the Nazis. The Home Guard was up and running. The Kelvin Hall became a major centre for the production of sea-rescue dinghies and barrage and convoy balloons. Glasgow, declared one member of the Government, was now 'the arsenal of the Empire'.

Women volunteered to work in the munitions factories or on the land. Many others joined the WRNS (Women's Royal Naval Service), the ATS (Auxiliary Territorial Service) or the WAAF (Women's Auxiliary Air Force). It has been estimated that, by 1943, more than 443,000 women were in uniform. Whether in uniform or in the factories, the women played a decisive role in the war effort at home.

THE END IS NIGH

Churchill desperately needed America's help in fighting the Nazis. On at least four occasions, he sailed across the Atlantic from Greenock in order to persuade the US President, Franklin D Roosevelt, to abandon its neutralist stance.

In 1941, Churchill brought Roosevelt's emissary, Harry Hopkins, to Britain, and his visitor was impressed by what he saw of the war effort. They ventured north, to Glasgow, and dined in a suite of what was then the North British Hotel, overlooking George Square. During the meal he informed Churchill and the other guests that he would return to Roosevelt and tell him, quoting from the bible, 'Wheresoever thou goest, we go and, where thou lodgest, we lodge; thy people shall be our people, thy God, our God, even unto the end.' Churchill, realising that America was a step closer to entering the war, wept. A plaque marking the occasion still stands in that suite, in what is now the Millennium Hotel.

The Second World War was fought out in many different arenas, at enormous human cost, over the next four years. Peace was a long time in arriving, but when it did, in May 1945, Britain's joy was unconfined. Glasgow's celebrations were every bit as jubilant and heart-felt as those anywhere else; and George Square witnessed an outpouring of relief that can never be replicated.

The sandbagged main entrance to the Glasgow Corporation Transport offices in Bath Street

A decontamination squad at work following a mock gas attack on Glasgow, 1941

Workmen demolishing unsafe buildings after an air-raid on Greenock in May 1941

A Clydebank family making their way through the devastated streets in search of temporary shelter after the Blitz in 1941

German POWs watched by Councillor McInnes, Glasgow Corporation Sub-convenor of Housing, at work on Pollok housing estate, where they are making roads and sewers

A Glasgow Home Guard unit staging a mock attack for the benefit of an army VIP who was visiting the city's Home Guard Town Fighting School

A rescue squad preparing to dig out a young woman who had been trapped for six days beneath rubble after the house had been flattened by German bombs during a night of multiple air-aids over Glasgow

A sign warning of a gas attack in September 1941. However it was only a mock attack, designed to test the city's readiness for the real thing

A bombed-out family gather on the street with their possessions, after German bombers flattened Clydebank in March 1941

The Home Guard practising shooting on the range

German POWs attend a service at Glasgow Cathedral in 1947

German POWs rescued from the *Bismark* arrive at Albert Dock, Greenock 1941

Home Guard members with 'bomb snuffers'. These were placed over incendiary bombs to prevent the spread of fire

Land Girls with their tools of the trade in a march during Glasgow's War Weapon Week, in November 1940

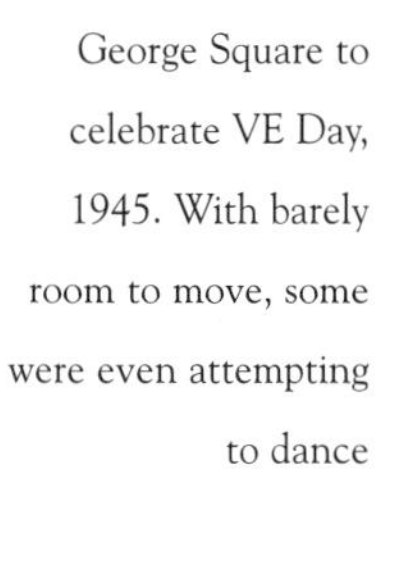

Crowds thronging George Square to celebrate VE Day, 1945. With barely room to move, some were even attempting to dance

Happy-looking survivors after the previous night's air raid

Rangers' John Greig and Celtic's Billy McNeill lead out the Old Firm for a 1968 derby

SPORT

Chapter Seven

SPORT

FOOTBALL

There are, just possibly, sports in the West of Scotland that have more adherents than football, but it is football that has the highest profile. From their bases in the East End and the Southside of Glasgow, Celtic and Rangers have exercised a grip over the Scottish game that is as unshakeable as the Kremlin. They have the most illustrious histories, the largest collections of silverware, the best players (by and large), the most luxurious stadia, the longest waiting-lists of fans eager to fill them. The last time the SPL title opportunistically ventured outwith Glasgow, it was to Aberdeen back in the year of Live Aid, in 1985. The slightest news of an impending Old Firm transfer commands pole position in the newspapers' back pages. These two clubs dominate Scottish football and their absence would leave an unfillable void.

Both sides have a seemingly inexhaustible gallery of great players: Jimmy Johnstone, Bobby Lennox, Tommy Gemmell, Bertie Auld, Billy McNeill, Patsy Gallacher, Jimmy McGrory, Kenny Dalglish; Jim Baxter, Willie Henderson, John Greig, Willie Woodburn, Jerry Dawson, Davie Meiklejohn, George Young, Davie Cooper. Glasgow and the West also has given rise to some of the finest and most effective managers ever seen in Britain: Jock Stein, Alex Ferguson, Bill Shankly, Matt Busby, Willie Waddell.

Then there is Hampden – the biggest football stadium in the world until 1950. In its days, it has claimed a good number of record attendances: 149,000 (149,000!) to see Scotland beat the Auld Enemy 3–1 in 1937; 146,000 for Celtic's Scottish Cup triumph over Aberdeen that same year; 136,000 for the Celtic–Leeds United European Cup semi-final, in 1970. Imagine those crowds today.

Hampden has seen great cup finals and innumerable home internationals, not to mention a game that has gone down as one of the finest of all time: the 1960 European Cup final between Real Madrid v Eintracht Frankfurt, which the magnificent Spaniards won, 7–3. The number of people who claim to have been there far exceeds the official attendance of 127,000, but no matter. For that match, and for others, the old stadium has served the Beautiful Game well.

BOXING

Glasgow's love affair with sport extends far beyond football to encompass everything from golf and rugby to swimming, boxing and bowls. And, in all of these sports and more, men and women from the West of Scotland have made their name at national (and, frequently, international) level.

Take boxing. Benny Lynch – who else could we have started off with? – was the wiry, tenacious figure from the Gorbals who has been romanticised ever since his premature death in August 1946, and is still seen as one of the greatest fighters Britain has ever produced. How often have we heard stories that a film is, finally, going to be made of his life? The chastening circumstances surrounding his decline and death have been rehearsed many times but it's worth recounting a personal memoir that surfaced a year or so ago from a doctor who was the registrar on duty the night that Lynch, near death, was brought to the city's Southern General Hospital.

The wee man was already well known to the staff through his frequent drink-related admissions. On his last night on earth (a suitably wet and miserable one) he was again brought in, and admitted to an acute medical ward. But nothing could be done to save him. The following day, the registrar glimpsed a crowd of men and women outside, waiting to pay their last respects. At length, a hearse emerged slowly and drove through the gates; bunnets were doffed and tears trickled down cheeks. The crowd departed in a sombre mood for home or pub. Fifteen minutes later, another hearse appeared – this time, the one carrying Lynch's coffin. It, too, emerged slowly but there was no-one there to pay any final respects.

One of Glasgow's greatest sporting nights came on April 17, 1979, at the Kelvin Hall. Nearly 10,000 fans were beside themselves at what was shaping up as a famous victory. In the ring, Jim Watt had been trading blows with Colombian Alfredo Pitalua for eleven rounds and, in the twelfth, Watt caught Pitalua with two right hooks to the head then stepped in with a decisive flurry of blows. The referee shot a glance at Pitalua and stopped the fight. Bedlam. Ten thousand shrieking voices nearly blew the roof off the Kelvin Hall: Watt had become the WBC lightweight champion. The newspaper reports the next day capture the excitement well. 'Million Dollar Daddy!' ran the headline in the *Evening Times*, above a photograph of Watt with his young daughter, Michelle. The report quoted the fight's co-promoter, Mickey Duff, as saying that Watt could expect to make a million dollars should everything go according to plan. Watt would go on to make four successful defences of his title before losing to the highly rated Nicaraguan, Alexis Arguello, at Wembley.

Beyond Watt and Lynch, there have been champion boxers like James Tancy Lee, Peter (P.K.) Keenan, Walter McGowan, Jackie Paterson, Vic Herman (who was also a noted artist and bagpiper), Jim Higgins, John 'Cowboy' McCormack, Jackie Brown and Chic Calderwood. There's a story about how Keenan once brought Cassius Clay (as he was at the time) to Paisley for an exhibition bout. Clay apparently declined to do much to publicise the bout so Keenan slapped him in the face. There aren't many people who would have done that.

Muhammad Ali visited Glasgow in November 1993 to promote a book that narrated the story of his career. The sheer thrill of being in the same room as someone as iconic as Ali is not something you easily forget. His Parkinson's was bad then but he still pulled out all the stops, and for a while the old magic returned. (A personal note: I found myself with Ali and some of

his entourage in a basement side-room in the old Waterstone's bookstore in Union Street. Someone gave him a sandwich but the filling – I can't remember what it was – had partially fallen on to his knee, and he stared it at dully. Gingerly, I picked it up and handed it back to him, thinking how small my hand looked next to his – that this was the hand that had flattened Joe Frazier. I also remember thinking, no-one will ever believe me if I told them what I have just done.)

MOTOR SPORT

In motor racing, who can forget Jackie Stewart, the brilliant three-times winner of the world championship? In similar rubber-burning mode, there was biker Bob McIntyre, the first man to lap the Isle of Man TT course at more than 100 mph.

ATHLETICS

In athletics, the West has given rise to such indomitable names as Frank Clement (fifth in the Olympic 1500m final in 1976), Tom McKean (four times winner of the European Cup 800m), Lachie Stewart (he unforgettably defeated the legendary Ron Clarke in the Commonwealth 10,000m race in Edinburgh in 1970), Cameron Sharp, Graham Williamson, Les Piggott, Joe McGhee.

GOLF

In golf, Colin Montgomerie has been one of the most familiar names on the circuit for years – although he's still in search of that elusive major. Sam Torrance is still remembered for that glorious winning putt to give Europe the Ryder Cup at the Belfry in 1985 (and for his equally triumphant victory salute). Belle Robertson is a true legend in Scottish ladies' golf, winning the British Ladies' Amateur in 1981, after finishing second so many times. Before them, there were people like Hammy McInally, who played off a one handicap with his right hand – and a three with his left.

CRICKET AND RUGBY

Like many Scottish schools, Ayr Academy prides itself on its sporting prowess. Its former pupils include Mike Denness, who made his name in English cricket, scoring more than 25,000 runs, captaining England in nineteen test matches and hitting four test centuries; and rugby hero Ian 'Mighty Mouse' McLauchlan, one-time Scotland captain and British Lion. Other rugby stars from the West have included prop Sandy Carmichael, another ex-Lion, Gordon Brown ('Broon fae Troon'), who died a few years ago, and his brother, Peter.

SWIMMING

From Lanarkshire there once came three female swimmers who dominated their sport in the post-war era. Helen Orr 'Elenor' Gordon and Cathy Gibson were Olympic bronze medallists and Nancy Riach, who was once described as the finest swimmer in the Empire, died at the age of twenty while swimming for Great Britain in Monte Carlo, a victim of polio.

OTHER SPORTS

In tennis, we've had people like Winnie Shaw, twice a quarter-finalist in the ladies' singles at Wimbledon and a semi-finalist (with Dundee's Joyce Hume) in the ladies' doubles. In bowls, there have been champions – and characters – like Bob Kissach, J C Irving and railway worker Jock McAtee. Weightlifting boasts Commonwealth champion John McNiven; in cycling, Robert Millar and Billy Bilsland are probably the West's best known names. In basketball, Willie Cameron was, at one time, the sport's most-capped British internationalist. In badminton, there was Dan Travers and, in horseracing, Sandy Barclay was the winner of three Classics. And when American baseball fans talk about the 'shot that was heard around the world', they are referring to a crucial home-run struck by Glasgow-born Jim Thomson during a 1951 National League play-off between the Jim's team, the New York Giants, and their arch-rivals, the Brooklyn Dodgers. Jim swung at the ball and hit it clean out of the park. It was one of the most famous moments in baseball – some say it even ranks, among New Yorkers, alongside the memory of John F Kennedy's assassination.

Some of these sportsmen and women from Glasgow and the West have faded into ill-deserved obscurity. Others will live on. Collectively, they remind you that, when it comes to producing champions, near-champions and larger-than-life characters, we certainly have been prolific.

Celtic manager Jock Stein hugs hat-trick hero John 'Dixie' Deans after Celtic's 6-1 Scottish Cup Final victory over Hibs in May 1972

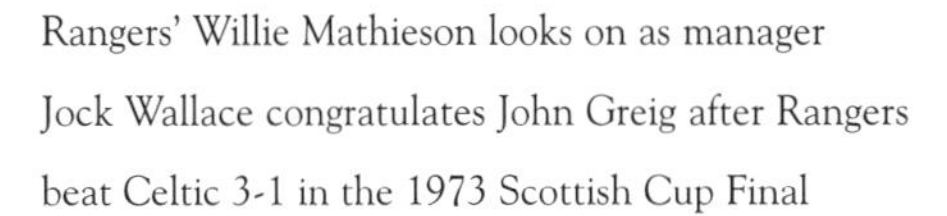

Rangers' Willie Mathieson looks on as manager Jock Wallace congratulates John Greig after Rangers beat Celtic 3-1 in the 1973 Scottish Cup Final

Celtic's Lou Macari declines the kind offer of a kiss from Rangers' Alex McDonald after an incident between the two during a 1970 Old Firm game

SO...BUY

SOUTH WEST STAND

A full house at Hampden in 1964

The famous aftermath of Scotland's 2-1 victory over England at Wembley Stadium in 1977. The Scots fans invaded the pitch and broke the goalposts

In the 1966 game at Hampden, Scotland's Denis Law, arms aloft, celebrates one of his two goals against the Auld Enemy

Matt Busby leading out Scotland against an English side captained by Joe Mercer at Hampden in 1951

Glasgow boxer Benny Lynch is watched by a large crowd as he trains in the ring

Jim Watt lets fly with a left, and Alfredo Pitalua counters with a body punch during the World Title fight in Glasgow, 1979

Muhammad Ali
during his visit to
Glasgow in 1965

World Champion racing driver Jackie Stewart at Glasgow Airport, 1975

Jackie Stewart driving a Matra through the rain at Oulton Park, 1975

A diver gives a spectacular display at Prestwick open air swimming pool, 1939

Scottish athlete Eric Liddell wins the Celtic Sports 120-yards sprint in August 1922

These two gents, in contrasting dress styles, keep a close eye on the runners at Ayr races in 1947

Over the jumps at Ayr Racecourse

6.

Glasgow Fair
luggage at Gourock
Pier, 1939

LEISURE

CHAPTER EIGHT

LEISURE

ARE YE DANCIN'?

A long while ago, a newspaper wrote of Glasgow that it teemed with 'cheap, low dancing places' where young people of both sexes met once or twice a week to 'dance, drink and enjoy themselves'. At a guess, you might think the description came from, say, the 1930s or maybe the 1940s. It came, in fact, from 1872, which only goes to show how some leisure pursuits in Scotland's biggest city have a long pedigree.

The quote actually referred to 'the youth of both sexes among the lower ranks of society', which might have given the game away. According to the *People's Palace Book of Glasgow*, the first purpose-built place for dancing in the city was established not long after French Revolution – in 1796, to be exact – at the Assembly Room in the Tontine Buildings. But only the richest people could afford to dance there. By the time of the Roaring Twenties, Glasgow had eleven ballrooms (three more than London) and around seventy other dance halls. The world economy might have been enduring a slump at the time but the only sensible response by the ordinary person was to have a good night out at the dancing. All sorts of new dances came and went during this era – the slow foxtrot, the rumba, the tango and the Charleston among them.

The interwar years saw a boom in the leisure field. By 1930, Glasgow had no fewer than 127 cinemas. The cavernous Green's Playhouse, in Renfield Street, opened in 1927 and it was said that around 6,000 dancers could dance the night away in its giant ballroom. As historian Irene Maver puts it, 'The need to seek glamorous horizons beyond the confines of crowded tenements was often put forward as a prime reason for the allure of the cinema and the dancing.'

An image that lingers to this day of some dance halls of that era comes from reading *No Mean City*, with its vivid (fictional) accounts of drink-fuelled, gang-related punch-ups that flared into life at the slightest provocation. But the more enduring image of the Glasgow dance hall is of a place where you could get a 'lumber' for the night and have fun with your friends. Even during the grim and uncertain years of the Second World War, the dance halls in Glasgow broke all sorts of attendance records – aided, no doubt, by the large numbers of American GIs and their fancy footwork.

In the mid 1950s, the manager of one city dance hall, a man who'd travelled widely in Europe and North America, said that he had never encountered anything like the Glaswegians' passion for dancing. He gazed upon several hundred young people dancing, each with an estimated eight square feet in which to show off his (or her) stuff. The men were mostly dressed in lounge suits

and bright ties, the women in new, short-sleeved dresses. Others watched from the sidelines, nibbling sandwiches and cake and sipping tea, coffee or lemonade.

The denizens of the dancehalls came from every trade and profession, from hospital staff-rooms and university lecture rooms to shipyards and factories, from single-ends to detached villas. It was estimated that someone attending the dancing four or five nights a week might spend £1 on admission and tea (£1, of course, was worth a lot more then that it is now). A typist could easily spend up to a fifth of her weekly pay on the dancing.

The dancers could be roughly divided into three groups: the sedate family parties and middle-class dancers, usually aged between their late twenties and forties; the late-teens to mid-twenties (some of them Teddy boys) who congregated in the big halls that could accommodate upwards of 1,500, drawn by midnight dancing sessions and free gifts; and thirdly, those whose rowdy behaviour would lead to regular appearances in the police courts. (In 1962, church representatives objected to a planned Sunday dance club at the Locarno, claiming that it would attract undesirable characters from a wide area and would also dilute the distinctive character of the Scottish Sabbath.)

Some dance halls employed bouncers to eject drunk or disorderly troublemakers. One enterprising hall employed a squad of girls dressed in short skirts and nylon stockings to distract would-be brawlers and hooligans. It paid off, naturally.

Many of the great dance halls are no longer with us but they live on in the memory – the Dennistoun Palais, the Locarno, the Majestic, the Berkeley, Green's Ballroom or the Albert. There are many couples around today who would never have come in contact with each other had not their eyes met across a crowded dance floor.

THE FLICKS

Further magic is conjured by the evocative names of the old cinemas that once graced the city – the Parade in Dennistoun, the Oxford Playhouse at Springburn, Possilpark Picture House, Crosshill Picture House, the Embassy in Shawlands, the Black Cat in Bridgeton, Cathcart Picture House, La Scala in Sauchiehall Street, the Seamore in Maryhill, the Rex in Riddrie and the Rio at Bearsden and at Rutherglen. But, as author Bruce Peter says in his book, *One Hundred Years of Glasgow's Amazing Cinemas*, a large number of these cinemas were cheaply built and didn't have much respect for their surroundings. On the other hand, they did have an immense impact on people's lives.

Glasgow's very first film-screening, primitive though it was, took place in May 1896, in Sauchiehall Street. It was enough to start a collective love-affair with cinema that has persisted throughout all the trends that have come and gone in films. By the time of the Second World War, the city had an estimated 114 cinemas, ranging from bedraggled fleapits to architectural marvels. The sights and the smells of the picture-house will forever remain with Glaswegians of a

certain age. Some people still maintain that it was possible to get in by handing over an empty jam-jar. They wouldn't get away with that now at their local UGC.

OTHER PURSUITS

Glasgow's art galleries and museums have always been popular, exerting a lasting influence on many who wandered round them on quiet weekends. Pub-culture deserves a book of its own, with venues like the Scotia, the Clutha Vaults and the Horseshoe all writing themselves into city legend. And who can overlook the roles played by restaurants and casinos in Glasgow's social life? Where the Royal Concert Hall and the Buchanan Galleries now stand, there used to be a Stakis venue, the Chevalier (named after Bonnie Prince Charlie), a £250,000 restaurant/casino complex with 'soft soundless carpets, muted lights and curtained walls'. It was a place designed with the swinging 60s in mind, with dinner, dancing and quality cabaret interspersed with gambling upstairs in what was, at the time, Britain's largest and most luxurious casino. Showbiz stars of the era, like singers Ronnie Carroll, Matt Munro and Cleo Laine, entertained the crowds.

Bingo, the greyhounds, the tea rooms, the bowling alleys, the circuses at the Kelvin Hall, the Crossmyloof ice rink, White City speedway at Ibrox (5000 spectators at the first meeting in 1928), climbing clubs, hiking, cycling and the weekly swim at the public baths – they have all had their devotees over the decades. Dorothy Paul, in her autobiography, writes about how she would meet up with her fellow cyclists at Renfrew Cross and race down to the roundabout at Greenock and back.

The city's public parks were conceived by the old Corporation as a means of giving Glaswegians somewhere to enjoy the fresh air and gentle exercise. By the 1930s, writes Irene Maver in her book, *Glasgow*, the 'Corpy' was responsible for no fewer than eight golf courses, twenty-two putting greens, twenty-five swimming pools, sixty-nine bowling greens, 131 tennis courts, nine cricket grounds, seventeen hockey pitches and 109 football pitches. It almost makes you wonder when Glaswegians found the time to ask, 'Are ye dancin?'

THE GLASGOW FAIR

The year is 1956. At Central Station, queues of families – the parents looking pale, laden with luggage and fidgety or over-excitable kids – are waiting for trains. Some trains are bound for Blackpool or Scarborough. But, for many people, the holidays mean going somewhere nearer home – 'doon the watter' to Rothesay, Millport, Largs, Ardrossan and Girvan.

The 50s were probably the last era in which this sort of holiday was the norm. In July 1964, though thousands of Glaswegians still headed for the Clyde coast or the Highlands, Fife or the Lothians, newspapers reported heavy bookings for resorts all over the Continent. That summer, BOAC (British Overseas Airways Corporation) introduced extra services between Prestwick and New York in response to demand.

As well as holidays 'doon the watter', the Glasgow Fair will forever be associated with pleasure trips on the *Waverley* and the *Queen Mary II*, sailings from the Broomielaw, donkey rides on the beach, the fabulous art-deco shorefront cafes, fish and chips in pokes, egg sandwiches covered in sand. It all seems far removed from the holiday situation today, when, in high summer, the airports are full of queues of families bound for Florida, Majorca or Cuba – the parents looking pale, and laden with luggage and fidgety or over-excitable kids.

A lack of swim-wear doesn't stop this gent enjoying a cooling paddle with two youngsters on Ayr beach in 1959

Pensioners on board the Clyde Steamer *Queen Mary II* as it leaves the Broomielaw, Glasgow for a sail Doon the Watter in the late 1950s

Typical Glasgow fair weather in 1965

Queues for the steamer at Rothesay Pier, 1945

John Henderson in his sou'wester and oilskins displays his catch at Dunoon in the 1950s

Betty Scott and Ruby Adam, both typists from Glasgow, enjoying themselves on the sands at Ayr, July 1953

Not an inch to
spare on the beach
at Rothesay, 1955

All the thrills of the 'Rotor' at the carnival at Glasgow Green in 1953

Betty Barclay of Anderston and Jimmy Campbell of Clydebank taking part in the twist competition at the Locarno in October 1962

CH
7

Calderpark Zoo in 1959, and 18-month-old Linda Sommerville from Bothwell gets a tiger by the tail

Chipperfield's Circus attracts the crowds in the Gorbals with its Elephant Parade, 1952

Katherine Hepburn relaxes after her performance in the title role of *The Millionairess* at the King's Theatre, Glasgow, in 1972

ENTERTAINMENT

CHAPTER NINE

ENTERTAINMENT

SPOILED FOR CHOICE

On an average day in 1912, you could choose from Fred Karno at the Empire Theatre, or Sir George Alexander's Company in *The Witness for the Defence* at the King's. If you didn't fancy those, you could always go to the Coliseum, the Palace, the Grand, the Princess, the Savoy or the Alhambra. The St Andrew's Halls and the City Halls were both popular venues for musical and other events. And there were picture-houses galore. No one can say that the Edwardian Glaswegian didn't know how to have a good time.

THE EMPIRE – WHERE SUCCESS MEANS NOT GETTING THE BIRD

It's only a small plaque, high up on the wall next to the Pizza Hut on Sauchiehall Street. You could walk past it every day for a year and not see it. But the plaque marks the spot of one of the greatest variety theatres Scotland has ever known – the Empire. Everyone played here. Frank Sinatra played the Empire, but his fortunes were at such a low ebb that he couldn't even sell it out. Chico Marx clowned on the stage. Judy Garland appeared here, as did Laurel and Hardy.

The Empire closed its doors in 1963 but lives on as the theatre that loved to give English comedians a hard time. Just ask Des O'Connor. He was part of a variety bill that also included a husband-and-wife variety act called Mackenzie Reid and Dorothy. A few days before opening night, Mackenzie was killed in a road accident, but his widow bravely decided to go on with the show, with her young nephew taking her husband's place. On the Thursday night, Dorothy suddenly burst into tears. She was unable to go on and Des, flustered, found himself propelled on to the stage, trying to break the theatre's mournful mood with a string of jokes, all of which fell flat. Seized by panic, he decided to end his agony by fainting. He was taken to Glasgow Royal Infirmary, but a doctor called his bluff.

Des was able to complete that night's second show, and the rest of the run. 'I left Glasgow bruised and battered, but wiser,' he wrote in his autobiography.

Morecambe and Wise once arrived at the Empire to the noise of a pneumatic drill at work outside. 'I know this is supposed to be the English comedians' graveyard,' quipped Eric, 'but I didn't know they dug your grave before you went on.'

Jon Pertwee, a one-time Dr Who, was a vaudeville comedian when he appeared at the Empire. He did his act to a deathly silence and walked off, his shoulders rounded in defeat. 'When I came off, I said to the manager, "Please sack me. Send me home because this is

disastrous." But he said I was a great success. A success? How did he make that out? Well, I hadn't got the bird, had I? Was that the criterion? Yes, it was, he assured me.' Poor Jon still had to get through another week at the Empire before he could return home.

The theatre had opened in 1897, occupying the site of the former Gaiety Theatre, and was extended in 1930 to seat 2,100. Because it was part of the huge Moss empire, it could attract all the stars who entertained at the London Palladium. Bob Bain, secretary of the Scottish Music Hall and Variety Theatre Society, has kept the Empire's memory alive in a dedicated website (www.freewebs.com/glasgow-empire). The Empire's roll-call, Bob says, included the giants of their day: Rosemary Clooney, Lena Horne, Ella Fitzgerald, Eartha Kitt, Frankie Laine, Johnnie Ray, Abbot and Costello, Dean Martin and Jerry Lewis, Mike and Bernie Winters, Danny Kaye, Howard Keel and Duke Ellington.

The sun set on the Empire on Sunday, March 31, 1963 (some say that the rise of independent TV was a factor) and an all-star cast bade farewell to the old place on a night of high emotion. Huge though it was, the Empire had always had lots of competition, right from the start. Some of the rival theatres – the Pavilion, the King's – live on today. Others were demolished and live on only in books and newspaper archives.

THE POTS AND PANS — THE PANOPTICON MUSIC HALL

Another, the Panopticon Music Hall on the Trongate, rich in history, has been saved and is being brought back to life. In January 2004, it staged a Celtic Connections show – its first live event since 1938. Stan Laurel and Jack Buchanan made their stage debuts at the Panopticon and it's often been claimed that the audiences would use elastic bands to fire rivets at acts they didn't like. Little wonder that the musicians in the orchestra demanded that a wire mesh be erected to protect their innocent heads.

THE PAVILION

The 1,800-seat Pavilion Theatre, which marked its centenary in 2004, has endured as the People's Theatre and, while never being the most fashionable haunt for Glasgow theatre-goers, it has prospered. Everyone has appeared here: Billy Connolly, Sheena Easton, Andy Cameron, Barbara Dickson, Lulu, Lex McLean, Harry Gordon, Chic Murray, Dave Willis, Jack Anthony, Tommy Morgan and Jack Milroy. The brilliant Tommy Morgan, from Bridgeton, did a record-breaking run of nineteen summer seasons at the Pavilion. Audiences could never get enough of him. When he died in 1961, it was revealed that he'd asked for his ashes to be scattered on the theatre's roof. His ghost is said to haunt the place to this very day.

The Pavilion, which is the last completely unsubsidised theatre in Scotland, even survived a rocky spell in the late 1970s but was saved by Iain Gordon, who has remained as general manager and has a knack for delivering what Glasgow audiences want in a popular theatre. *Paras Over the*

Barras, *Pride of the Clyde*, Dorothy Paul retrospectives, Billy Connolly plays, *Please Stay!*, Christmas pantos and the Mrs Brown trilogy have all been huge successes, helping to lure people from their TV sets and into the live theatre.

THE KING'S

The King's also celebrated its centenary in 2004. When it opened, it was said to be one of the most brilliant designs of the prolific theatre architect, Frank Matcham. He designed at least eighty others across the UK, including Glasgow's Empire.

In the 1930s the King's drama productions attracted actors of the calibre of Donald Wolfit, Gertrude Lawrence, Rex Harrison and Douglas Fairbanks Jnr. Hollywood stars, such as Katharine Hepburn, Vivien Leigh, Laurence Olivier, Alec Guinness, Tyrone Power and Sean Connery, also found themselves in its dressing-rooms.

The King's famed *Half Past Eight* summer shows ran between 1933 and 1947 and would often run for up to twenty-six weeks at a time. Not even the war could stop them. Harry Gordon, Beryl Reid, Dave Willis and the Tiller Girls were among the acts that appeared. The shows were relaunched as the *Half Past Seven* shows in 1961, with a new generation of comedians.

In the 1950s, Rikki Fulton and Jack Milroy performed a comedy sketch at the King's featuring two characters by the names of Francie and Josie and gave birth to a double act that became a Glasgow comedy legend. The King's, which is also famous for its pantos, was the setting for the Royal Variety Performance in 1977 to mark the Queen's Silver Jubilee visit to Scotland and the bill included The Jacksons and Dolly Parton. And Des O'Connor recalls how, on his last visit to Glasgow, he did his one-man act at the King's and, at the end, he had to hold back the tears as the entire audience sang 'Will Ye No' Come Back Again?' The memory of his faint at the Empire had been truly buried.

THE ALHAMBRA

The long-lost Alhambra, on Waterloo Street, was demolished in 1969, having been famous for its lavish *Five Past Eight* shows and pantos. Jimmy Logan, Stanley Baxter, Rikki Fulton, Jack Milroy, Max Bygraves and Cilla Black were among the stars who graced the stage. The extrovert American actress, Tallulah Bankhead, once shocked patrons by appearing on stage in her underwear.

THE CONCERT HALLS

Glasgow's number of concert venues has been no less prolific than its number of theatres. The old Green's Playhouse started as a cinema (said to be the largest in Europe) before attracting some of the top orchestras of the day. In 1973, it was renamed as the Glasgow Apollo. The Apollo attracted everyone from the Rolling Stones to Diana Ross before it finally closed its doors, after a concert by the Style Council, in 1985. The derelict building was torn down in the late 80s but, with the site now occupied by a towering UGC cinema, it continues to be a place of public entertainment.

The Barrowlands is another famous institution, having doubled as a dancehall and as an evocative concert venue, and attracted stars ranging from David Bowie and Blur to REM and U2. Other notable concert halls have included the City Halls in Candleriggs, the St Andrews Halls (gutted by fire in 1962), and the Plaza, at Eglinton Toll, which was for a long time also one of the city's favourite dancehalls.

Glasgow has a surfeit of entertainment memories – from the great days of the theatres and the concert halls, to the Beatles playing the Renfield Street Odeon. And we can also boast of the only time that Elvis Presley set foot in Britain. Granted, he never performed a concert here, but he did put in a fleeting appearance at Prestwick Airport in March, 1960.

Norman Wisdom in a scene from *Where's Charlie?* at the King's Theatre, Glasgow 1957

Tyrone Power in *The Devil's Disciple* at the King's Theatre, Glasgow 1956

Frank Finlay in *The Long and the Short and the Tall* at the King's Theatre, Glasgow 1959

Bandleader Duke Ellington in Glasgow for a performance in the late 1960s

Bob Hope carries singer Yana from the plane after arriving at Renfrew Airport, 1956

Comedy duo Laurel and Hardy bump into old friend Jack Graham at the Empire Theatre in Glasgow in 1954. They had known Jack when he was a member of the Dixie Minstrels

Cliff Richard in his dressing room at the Empire Theatre in 1959. Four prizewinners of a *Junior Times* competition won the privilege of meeting Cliff. With Cliff from left to right are: Ann McLean, Douglas Gordon, Rita Traynor and Neil Ritchie.

The *Half Past Seven* show at the King's Theatre, Glasgow, in 1962. Rikki Fulton and Jack Milroy with Gillian Lynne and Ethel Scott

Comedian Billy Connolly –
in typically irreverent mode

Charlie Chaplin poses for *The Bulletin* in his suite at the Ritz, 1921. At this time, Chaplin's audiences would not have seen his films, such as *City Lights* and *The Great Dictator* and, like his fellow Hollwood stars, he knew the promotional value of music hall appearances around the country, including Glasgow

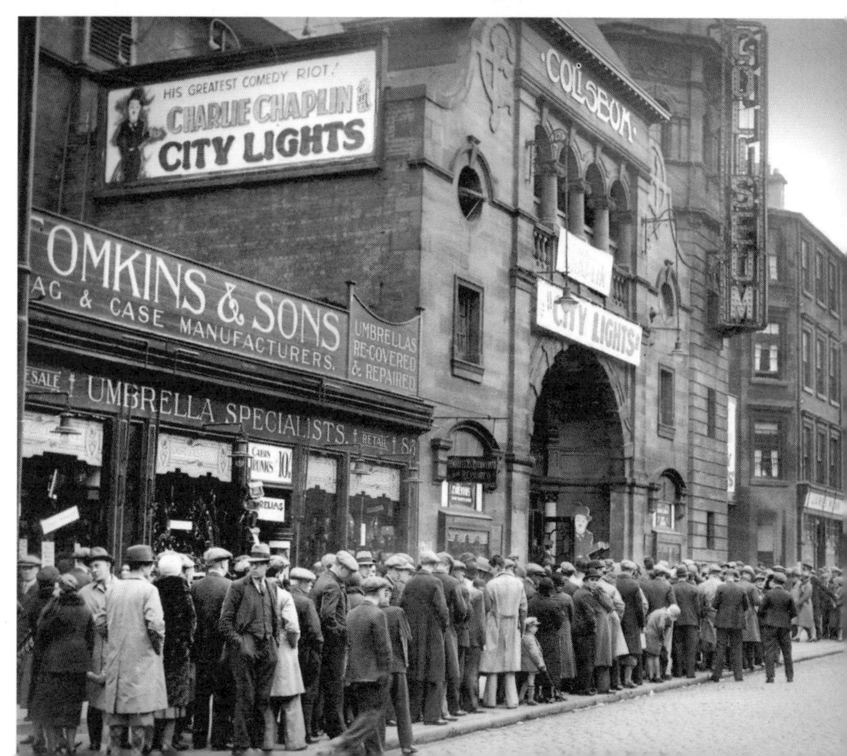

People queue outside the Coliseum cinema in Eglinton Street to see the Charlie Chaplin film *City Lights*

Fans with Elvis Presley at Prestwick Airport, March 1960

Judy Garland
during a visit to
Glasgow in 1963

Michael Caine as he appears in *The Long and The Short and the Tall* at the King's Theatre, Glasgow, 1959

Danny Kaye during his visit to Glasgow firm Letters where he had a set of golf clubs made for him in 1949

During his 1954 visit to Glasgow fans presented Nat King Cole with these pipes to add to his collection

Girls in curlers and plastic coats wait to see the Beatles in Glasgow, 1965

Ringo Starr and John Lennon of the Beatles at the Odeon cinema in Glasgow, 1965

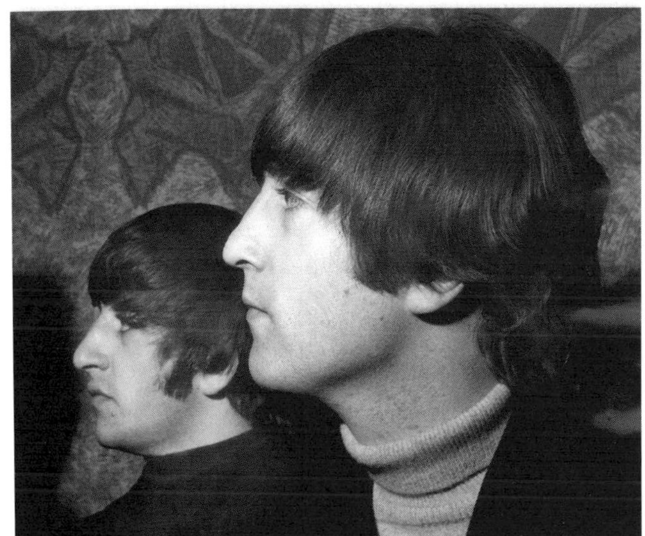

BIBLIOGRAPHY

BOOKS

Allen, Martin, *The Hitler/Hess Deception* (London: HarperCollinsPublishers, paperback edition, 2004)

Benson, Harry, *Harry Benson: Fifty Years in Pictures* (New York: Harry N Abrams Inc., 2001)

Carnegie, Liz, et al., *The People's Palace Book of Glasgow* (Edinburgh: Mainstream, 1998)

Clydebank Life Story Group, *Untold Stories: Remembering Clydebank in War Time* (Clydebank: Clydebank Life Story Group, 1999)

Devine, T M and **R J Findlay** (eds), *Scotland in the 20th Century* (Edinburgh: Edinburgh University Press, 1996)

Fahey, Jean *Up Oor Close: Memories of Domestic Life in Glasgow Tenements 1910–1945* (Oxford: White Cockade, in association with Springburn Museum Trust, 1998, first published 1990)

Fisher, Joe, *The Glasgow Encylopedia* (Edinburgh: Mainstream, 1994)

Fraser, W Hamish and **Irene Maver** (eds), *Glasgow, Volume II: 1830 to 1912* (Manchester: Manchester University Press, 1996)

Gilbert, Martin, *Churchill: A Life* (London: Pimlico, 2000)

Hurst, K A, *William Beardmore: Transport is the Thing* (Edinburgh: National Museums of Scotland, 2004)

Johnston, Ian, *Ships for a Nation, 1847–1971: John Brown & Company, Clydebank* (West Dunbartonshire Libraries and Museums, 2000)

Keating, Michael, *The City that Refused to Die* (Aberdeen: Aberdeen University Press, 1988)

MacPhail, I M M, *The Clydebank Blitz* (Clydebank: West Dunbartonshire Libraries and Museums, 2000; first published 1974)

McArthur, A and **H Kingsley Long**, *No Mean City* (London: Corgi Adult, 1969)

McGinn, Matt, with **Hamish Whyte** (ed.), *McGinn of the Calton: The Life and Works of Matt McGinn 1928–1977* (Glasgow: Glasgow City Libraries Publications, 1987)

Maver, Irene, *Glasgow* (Edinburgh: Edinburgh University Press, 2000)

Morton, H V, *In Search of Scotland* (London: Methuen, 2000; first published 1934)

Oakley, C A, *The Second City* (Glasgow: Blackie & Son, 1947; first published 1946)

O'Connor, Des, *Bananas Can't Fly: The Autobiography* (London: Headline, 2002)

Osborne, Brian D and **Ronald Armstrong** (eds), *Mungo's City: A Glasgow Anthology* (Edinburgh: Birlinn, 1999)

Paul, Dorothy, *Dorothy: Revelations of a Rejected Soprano* (Edinburgh: Mainstream, 2002)

Peter, Bruce, *One Hundred Years of Glasgow's Amazing Cinemas* (Edinburgh: Polygon, 1996)

Robertson, Seona and **Les Wilson**, *Scotland's War* (Edinburgh: Mainstream, 1995)

Stephenson, Pamela, *Billy* (London: HarperCollinsEntertainment, 2001)

'No Mean Society': *200 Years of the Royal Philosophical Society of Glasgow* (Glasgow: The Royal Philosophical Society of Glasgow, 2003)

NEWSPAPERS

Archives of the *Evening Times* and *The Herald*

ACKNOWLEDGEMENTS

Thanks to Jean Fahey, Bob Bain, Ken McNab and Sheila Hamilton for their help. All errors are the author's.

Russell Leadbetter is deputy features editor at the *Evening Times* in Glasgow. He has also written *You Don't Have to Be in Harlem*, the story of the Glasgow Apollo.

Rod Sibbald is Picture Editor at Newsquest in Glasgow, owners of the *Evening Times*.

TIMES PAST

THE STORY OF GLASGOW

'In a city known for its poor housing and hard industries, Glaswegians had to make the most of any free time that came their way.'

'Ladies found a refuge in Miss Cranston's Tea Room while the men took time to relax in the pub.'

BLACK & WHITE PUBLISHING

TIMES PAST: THE STORY OF GLASGOW is a beautifully illustrated volume which includes many spectacular and previously unpublished photographs of the city, brought together here for the first time. Based on the hugely popular *Evening Times* supplement, *Times Past* is a nostalgic and heart-warming look at the city, with specially written introductions to each chapter by *Evening Times* journalist Russell Leadbetter.

With chapters on Growing Up in Glasgow, Daily Life, Shipbuilding, Entertainment, the War Years, Holidays Doon the Watter and more, *Times Past: The Story of Glasgow* covers all aspects of the 'Second City of the Empire' and tells the remarkable story of the city and its people through carefully selected images from the *Evening Times*' own archive.

ISBN 1-84502-029-4
9 781845 020293 >

£12.99